VALENTINE'S DAY

Joanna Ponto

Enslow Publishing
101 W. 23rd Street
Suite 240
New York, NY 10011
USA

enslow.com

Published in 2016 by Enslow Publishing, LLC.
101 W. 23rd Street, Suite 240, New York, NY 10011

Library of Congress Cataloging-in-Publication Data

Ponto, Joanna.
  Valentine's Day / Joanna Ponto.
     pages cm. — (The story of our holidays)
  Includes bibliographical references and index.
  ISBN 978-0-7660-7462-0 (library binding)
  ISBN 978-0-7660-7474-3 (pbk.)
  ISBN 978-0-7660-7468-2 (6-pack)
  1. Valentine's Day—Juvenile literature. I. Title.
GT4925.P66 2016
394.2618—dc23
                                    2015031593

Printed in the United States of America

To Our Readers: We have done our best to make sure all website addresses in this book were active and appropriate when we went to press. However, the author and the publisher have no control over and assume no liability for the material available on those websites or on any websites they may link to. Any comments or suggestions can be sent by e-mail to customerservice@enslow.com.

Portions of this book originally appeared in the book *Valentine's Day: Candy, Love, and Hearts.*

Photos Credits: Cover, p. 1 stockcreations/Shutterstock.com; p. 4 Anke van Wyk/Shutterstock.com; p. 6 Amanda Dumouchelle/iStock/Thinkstock; p. 9 Private Collection/Archives Charmet/Bridgeman Images; p. 11 WDG Photo/Shutterstock.com; p. 15 Photolibrary/Getty Images; p. 16 iStock.com/ Pamela Moore; p. 19 Suslik1983/Shutterstock.com; p. 21 Gabe Ginsberg/FilmMagic/Getty Images; p. 22 Linda Davidson/The Washington Post/Getty Images; p. 24 Joe Amon/The Denver Post/Getty Images; p. 27 Ammodramus/Wikimedia Commons/Valentine, Nebraska street sign.jpg/public domain; pp. 28–29 Karen Huang.

Contents

All kinds of holidays and occasions call for greeting cards!
Cards are fun to receive in the mail.

Chapter 1

A Card for Every Occasion

Greeting cards are available for all kinds of occasions. There are cards for birthdays, weddings, and school graduations. Cards bring good wishes and show that we care.

Cards are also often sent on holidays. Millions of Christmas cards are mailed each year. Halloween cards are always fun to send. But we do not give cards on every holiday. Usually, cards are not sent on holidays such as Columbus Day, Washington's Birthday, or Martin Luther King Jr. Day.

Cards for Love

There is one holiday especially known for cards. These cards have words about love or friendship. Often they are red or

Sending Some Love

It is fun to give cards to all your friends and family on Valentine's Day. You can buy cards at the store, but it is even more fun to make your own!

pink. Some have hearts on them. They are called valentines. Many people make their own valentines. Other people buy them in stores.

You can give a valentine to anyone you care about. Children may give them to friends. Parents may give them to their children. Grandparents may give them to their grandchildren. Some people even give their pets valentines.

People send valentines each year on February 14, Valentine's Day. It is not the same kind of holiday as Presidents' Day. Schools are open on Valentine's Day. So are banks and businesses. Mail carriers are especially busy that day. They deliver tons of valentines.

Valentine's Day is a special time. It is a day for friendship and caring. It is a holiday about love.

Chapter 2

The First Celebrations

Valentine's Day is an old celebration. People have celebrated it for hundreds of years. Yet no one is sure exactly how Valentine's Day started.

A Roman God

It may have started with the ancient Romans. They lived more than two thousand years ago in the country of Italy. Each year on February 15, they held a special celebration known as the festival of Lupercalia. The festival honored the Roman god Lupercus. The Romans believed that Lupercus protected them from wolves.

Everyone enjoyed the festival. People danced and sang. There were footraces, and people played games for hours.

When in Rome

Valentine's Day is believed to have come from the time of the ancient Romans. Each year on February 15, the Romans would have a big festival to honor the god Lupercus, who was thought to protect everyone from wolves.

One game was a way for young people to meet. It began the night before the festival. On the evening of February 14, the girls gathered together. They wrote their names on pieces of paper. The papers were put into a large bowl.

Each boy picked a paper from the bowl. He could not peek at the name on it. The girl whose name he picked would be his partner during the festival. All the couples spent the day together. Some fell in love and later married.

A Priest Named Valentine

Many people believe that Valentine's Day started differently. They think it may have started with two priests. Both men were named Valentine.

This story also takes place in ancient Rome in the third century CE. Claudius II, the emperor, was a cruel ruler. He wanted Christians to give up their religion. He told them to pray to the Roman gods. Those who refused were jailed or even killed.

A priest named Valentine would not obey. He was put in jail. The children missed their priest a lot. They passed notes to Valentine through the jail window, and he wrote back to them. Valentine became friendly with the jailer's daughter. She was a blind girl who brought Valentine his food.

Even in jail, Valentine was not safe from Claudius II. The emperor again ordered Valentine to pray to the Roman gods. The priest refused, and he was killed on February 14.

Valentine wrote one last note to the jailer's daughter before he died. According to the story, the blind girl was able to read the note. She could see again.

Valentine may have written the first Valentine's Day card.

The priest wrote on the note, "From Your Valentine." Some say that is why we send valentines today.

Another Valentine Story

But is it? There is a story about another priest named Valentine. He also stood up to Emperor Claudius II but for a different reason.

Claudius II had wanted to build a powerful army. He ordered his soldiers not to marry. The emperor did not want the men to think about their families. He wanted them to think only about winning battles.

Claudius II warned priests not to marry people. But Valentine did not listen. He married young couples anyway and was arrested. Claudius II had him killed on February 14.

Some people think both stories are true. But they believe the stories are about the same man. Was there only one Valentine? We may never know.

Perhaps one priest named Valentine did many good things. Maybe he refused to pray to the Roman gods. He may have also helped young lovers to marry. And he could have been a friend to children. Valentine was later made a saint.

Love Is for the Birds

But wait, the story is not over. There is still another tale about how Valentine's Day may have started. This one began long ago in England. People there noticed that many birds picked their mates around February 14. They felt that people should do the same. So February 14 became a day for love.

Which Valentine's Day story is true? In some ways they may all be. Boys picked girls' names out of a bowl during Lupercalia. Today,

Some birds, such as swans, pick their mates around February 14.

schoolchildren do something like that. At parties they often pick valentines out of a box.

A priest named Valentine sent kind notes. Now people send Valentine's Day cards. Birds are still a part of Valentine's Day, too. Lovebirds make us think of love. They are often seen on Valentine's Day cards. Valentine's Day is probably a mix of many different stories and ideas.

It is fun to think about how Valentine's Day may have started. It is even more fun to celebrate it.

Chapter 3

Celebrations Across the United States

Americans everywhere celebrate Valentine's Day. Many people send cards. This idea began in America in the mid-1700s. Most of the early valentines were homemade.

Early American Valentines

Valentines really became popular in the early 1900s. By then, there were large greeting card companies. People could buy nice cards at low prices. There were even penny valentines. Children especially liked these. They gave them to their friends.

There was another reason valentines became popular. It had nothing to do with love or friendship. It was because of

Cards for the Blind

Some Valentine's Day cards are specially made for people who cannot see to read them. They are written in braille. Braille is a language using raised dots that people can read with their fingers.

the mail service. In 1790, there were only about seventy-five post offices in the United States. By 1900, there were more than seventy-five thousand. This made it easier to send valentines. People anywhere could receive them.

Today you can find all kinds of valentines. Some are even musical. When one of these is opened, a song plays. Some valentine cards are large. They are so big they may not fit in the mailbox. The mail carrier might have to bring them directly to the door.

There are cards with long love poems or short, funny sayings. Americans spend about $277 million on valentines every year. The only holiday that people spend more on cards is Christmas.

Hearts, Cupids, and Lovebirds

Hearts, cupids, and lovebirds are Valentine's Day symbols. They stand for things we think of on Valentine's Day. Hearts stand for the love people show on Valentine's Day. Cupid is the Roman god of love. He has wings and a bow and arrow. Cupid's arrow stands for love. Anyone hit by Cupid's arrow falls in love. Lovebirds stand for romance. This goes along with the old belief that birds mate on February 14.

Often, schools have Valentine's Day celebrations. Students might decorate their classrooms. Many also make Valentine's Day cards.

People started sending lots of valentines in the early 1900s. Many companies made good cards at low prices.

Many people make cards themselves. They use colored paper, such as red or pink, for Valentine's Day.

They might cut out hearts, cupids, and lovebirds. Usually red or pink paper is used. These are Valentine's Day colors.

Children often give one another valentine cards at school parties. Special Valentine's Day treats might also be served. There will probably be cookies in the shape of hearts. Cupcakes with pink icing, chocolates wrapped in red foil, chocolate-covered strawberries, and small heart-shaped sugar candies with Valentine's Day sayings on them are all popular treats.

Some schools and clubs have Valentine's Day dances. There are Valentine's Day fairs, too. At these, clowns do face painting. They might paint hearts and cupids on children's cheeks.

Valentine's Day games are fun. People might toss a heart-shaped beanbag or guess the number of pink-and-red jellybeans in a big jar. Valentine's Day foods are also always sold. The heart-shaped pizzas are delicious. There will be lots of pink and red desserts, as well.

Most public libraries celebrate Valentine's Day. Often, the children's room is decorated for the holiday. Children's books about Valentine's Day are put on display. Sometimes special bookmarks are given out. These might list books for holiday reading. Many libraries offer Valentine's Day programs. A children's theater group might perform. There might also be a Valentine's Day arts and crafts time.

But not only children celebrate Valentine's Day. Adults enjoy cards and candy, too. Millions of heart-shaped boxes of chocolate are given. Often, flowers are also sent.

Some children give their parents helpful Valentines. These are more than cards. They are also gifts. The children decorate paper hearts. On them, they write something they will do to help their parents. They might write: "This valentine is good for one week of dog walking." A week of dish washing is another good choice. Parents love getting these. So do grandparents. But helpful valentines can be for anyone.

Kindness

Many young people try to make Valentine's Day extra special. They use the day to be a better friend or to do something kind. They can also thank someone who was nice.

Some students make valentines for people who might not get one. They may give a beautiful card to the school crossing guard. The janitor or school nurse might get one, too.

Sometimes a whole class might work on one large valentine. It could be given to a local fire station. Firefighters and police officers protect the community. Valentine's Day is a day to show that we care. Class valentines can also go to children in a hospital. People in nursing homes like getting them, too. Valentine cards make everyone feel good.

Kindness has no limits. Valentine's Day is a good time to prove that.

Valentine's Day Chocolate-Covered Strawberries*

Ingredients:

1 pint strawberries, washed and patted dry with paper towels

6 oz (135 g) bittersweet chocolate chips or baking chocolate

coarse sea salt (optional)

Directions:

1. In a microwave-safe bowl, place the chocolate chips. Microwave at half-power for 30 seconds or until the chocolate starts to melt. Stop the microwave and stir the chocolate. Repeat this, microwaving the chocolate for only about 30 seconds at a time.

2. Meanwhile, cover a cookie sheet in parchment or waxed paper.

3. As soon as the chocolate has melted, pull the bowl out of the pot (using oven mitts!) so the chocolate doesn't burn.

4. Holding the strawberry gently by the leaves or stem, dip the strawberry into the melted chocolate and roll it so the strawberry gets completely covered.

5. Place strawberry immediately onto the cookie sheet.

6. Repeat until all the strawberries are covered, placing them ½ inch apart so they don't touch.

7. Sprinkle sea salt onto chocolate, if desired.

8. Place in refrigerator for 1 to 2 hours or until chocolate has hardened.

9. Share these sweet treats with someone you love!

* Adult supervision required.

Chapter 4

Saying "I Do" on Valentine's Day

Valentine's Day is a perfect day to show some love. It is also a day for weddings. Every year, thousands of couples get married on February 14.

Love in Las Vegas

Chapels across the country are busy on Valentine's Day. Many couples flock to our nation's wedding capital. That is Las Vegas, Nevada.

There are more than fifty wedding chapels in Las Vegas. On Valentine's Day, many are open around the clock. Some have a wedding every fifteen minutes. Often, Las Vegas Valentine's Day weddings are highly creative and unusual.

This couple will always remember getting married on Valentine's Day.

One couple was married on a ship. The ship was docked in front of the Treasure Island Casino. A crew dressed as sailors and pirates were on hand for the ceremony. Another couple was wed at the Harley-Davidson Café. After the ceremony, they hopped on their motorcycles. The bride and groom rode around the city to celebrate. In still another ceremony, the couple said their vows in a hot air balloon!

Lots of people get married on Valentine's Day. These two people were married by an actor playing Elvis Presley!

A Las Vegas group wedding was held in a museum of wax figures. A number of couples were married at the same time. Wax figures were placed among the brides and grooms. These looked very real. It was hard to tell the wax figures from the real couples!

Love Around the World

Unusual Valentine's Day weddings are not just in Las Vegas. Some people have gone to Thailand for this. One year, thirty-six couples had a group wedding there.

It was an underwater event. The couples wore wedding clothes over their diving gear. They exchanged rings beneath the sea. The brides and grooms signed waterproof marriage documents. They used special pens for this.

All these couples had unforgettable weddings. For them, Valentine's Day will always be extra special.

Chapter 5

Creative City Celebrations

Certain cities celebrate Valentine's Day throughout the town. That happens each year in Loveland, Colorado. Loveland's nickname is The Sweetheart City. On Valentine's Day, the city lives up to its name and its nickname.

Zip Code of Love

The fun starts at the Loveland post office. Valentines mailed through Loveland get special treatment. They are stamped with a short valentine poem.

Loveland's post office does even more for the holiday. It has a Valentine re-mailing program. People from around the world take part. They send their valentines to the Loveland post

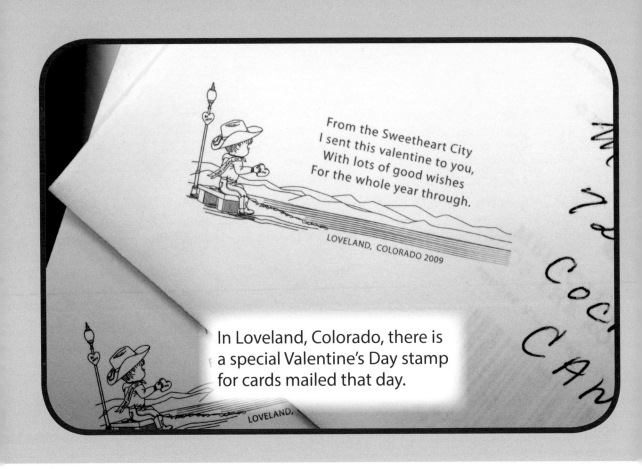

From the Sweetheart City
I sent this valentine to you,
With lots of good wishes
For the whole year through.

LOVELAND, COLORADO 2009

In Loveland, Colorado, there is a special Valentine's Day stamp for cards mailed that day.

office. The special stamp with the poem is added. Then the cards are sent on their way.

The town also has a holiday contest to pick a Miss Loveland Valentine. She will be Miss Loveland Valentine for one year.

The winner is always a student from the high school. The judges look for a special girl. She must have good grades. But personality is important, too.

Miss Loveland Valentine is kept busy. She attends all the town's events. She even visits the state's governor.

Boys are not left out of the fun. Each year a young boy is picked to be Cowboy Cupid. He is usually between four and six years old. Cowboy Cupid also goes to town celebrations. He is never hard to spot. He wears a cowboy outfit and, just like Cupid, he carries a bow and arrow.

The town is also decorated in pink and red for the holiday. Businesses hang hearts or cupids outside their buildings. Valentine's Day cards are hung between lampposts.

Valentines on the Internet

A fun way to send valentines is over the Internet. Many websites offer cards that you can send for free.

A City with Heart

Other towns celebrate in a big way, too. That is true of Valentine, Nebraska. It is known as America's Heart City. Each year, the Heart City has special Valentine celebrations. One is the Valentine's Day Coronation. At real coronations, kings and queens are crowned. Valentine, Nebraska, crowns a king and queen of hearts.

Everyone knows the royal couple. They are students from Valentine's Rural High School. Their classmates vote to choose them. They also vote for members of the Royal Valentine Court. This includes a prince and princess of hearts. There is a duke and duchess of hearts, as well.

Valentine, Nebraska, has held the coronation for more than fifty-five years. It is always on the Sunday before Valentine's Day. Many people come to see it. The high school band plays music. Students sing. High school students have a dance. Younger students also help with the ceremony. In fact, young people from kindergarten through high school take part. It is a fun time for everyone.

The Heart City has other celebrations, as well. These are not all for young people. At the Sweetheart Festival, couples married for fifty years or more are honored. A senior Valentine king and queen are crowned. In America's Heart City, Valentine's Day is for people of all ages—young and old.

Valentine's Day may be extra special in Valentine, Nebraska. The same goes for Loveland, Colorado. But this holiday can be terrific anywhere. It is a day for love and friendship. These are things for people everywhere to share.

These street signs in Valentine, Nebraska, show the city's love! It is called the Heart City.

Valentine's Day Craft

On Valentine's Day, you can have a special celebration besides sending cards. Try making these fun heart-shaped people to give out to loved ones or to decorate with.

Here are the supplies you will need:

2 sheets red construction paper
2 sheets pink construction paper
1 sheet white construction paper
15 small assorted hearts
glue
safety scissors

Directions:

1. Cut out two large hearts: one pink and one red.
2. Cut out four small hearts: two pink and two red.
3. Glue the bottom of the large red heart to the bottom of the large pink heart.
4. Cut the white paper into four 2½ inch by 10 inch strips.
5. Fold each strip back and forth like an accordion.
6. Glue the small red hearts to two of the white strips. Glue the small pink hearts to the other two strips.
7. Attach the strips to the body (made up of the two large hearts) to make arms and legs. Arrange the small assorted hearts to make a face. Glue these pieces together.

8. Let your heart person dry for 15 minutes, then display it for everyone to see!

Make Heart People Valentines

*Safety Note: Be sure to ask for help from an adult, if needed, to complete this project.

Glossary

braille—A language using raised dots that is read by using one's fingers.

community—A group of people living in the same area. A neighborhood is one type of community.

coronation—The crowning of a leader, such as a king or queen.

Claudius II—A Roman emperor who ruled during the third century CE.

Cupid—The Roman god of love.

Lupercalia—An ancient Roman festival.

penny valentines—Valentine's Day cards that cost one cent.

popular—Well liked.

symbol—Something that stands for something else.

Valentine—The Roman priest who was made a saint. Valentine's Day is named after him. A valentine can also be a card given on Valentine's Day.

Learn More

Books

Hayes, Amy. *Celebrate Valentine's Day.* New York: Cavendish Square Publishing, 2014.

Hibbert, Claire. *Terrible Tales of Ancient Rome.* New York: Gareth Stevens Publishing, 2014.

Owen, Ruth. *More Valentine's Day Origami.* New York: Rosen Publishing, 2014.

Owen, Ruth. *Valentine's Day Sweets and Treats.* New York: Windmill Books, 2012.

Websites

All About Valentine's Day for Kids and Teachers
kiddyhouse.com/Valentines
Check out Valentine's Day crafts, coloring pages, poems, and more at this fun website.

History of Valentine's Day
primarygames.com/holidays/valentines/history.php
Learn about how Valentine's Day got started with games, photos, and more.

Valentine, Nebraska: Everything About Valentine City
heartcity.net
Learn all about the history of this city.

Index